I0529008

World Headquarters

Books by Peter Fortunato

Poetry
A Bell or A Hook
Letters to Tiohero
Late Morning: New and Selected Poems
Entering the Mountain

Novel
Carnevale

Memoir
Desert Wind: My Life in Qatar

For Children
Color Me Earth

World Headquarters

Peter Fortunato

Fomite
Burlington VT

Copyright © 2024 Peter Fortunato
Cover image: detail of the painting "Galactic 1" by Peter Fortunato

All rights reserved. No part of this book may be may reproduced in any form or by any means
without the prior written consent of the publisher, except in the case of brief quotations and
reviews and certain other noncommercial uses permitted by copyright law.

ISBN-13: 978-1-959984-51-1
Library of Congress Control Number: 2024934698

Fomite
58 Peru Street
Burlington, VT 05401
9/1/2024

All experiences and life-forms cannot be proven to exist independently of their being a presence before your mind, just like a lucid dream.

—Longchenpa

Contents

I
World Headquarters

II
ad-Dawḥa

III
My Field

I

World Headquarters

For Those Lost at Sea

Catching myself at the edge of a whirlpool,
scanning the funnel of wrack and ruin, cautious
my mind might slip into wrath and commence
a monologue enumerating his lies,
his ignorance, the horrors well-documented,
and those on the horizon where Ocean ends
and Chaos reigns—the catastrophes before us,
our ship of state so badly steered,
captain and crew so ill-equipped,
even as a chorus continues its praise
while thunder opens the heavens above,
I ask instead how we have strayed so far,
worse than rudderless, our course plotted
by a man, hardly a man and more of an infant
constantly mewling he is blameless,
his incompetence always the fault of others?
Oh, what god is at work in this?
What god have we offended?
Antichrist might be an apt metaphor, but that
is a superstition of those who read literally
a book stitched from ancient prophecies—
oh, where will we find a hoary tale to consult
as map and source of inspiration while
under the strain to maintain our footing,
boat heaving, timbers cracking,
a few stalwarts on deck hold to hope
and loosen the sheets to cage a fair wind?
I am no sailor, soothsayer, nor rabble rouser,
no denier of any faith whose fruit is justice,
but a poet, who, like a child believes in dreams,
and after nightmares, in daylight sees what's plain:
he has no clothes to cover him,
he's witless and worse, and his sycophants
awful who worship him in fear and in greed,

hapless on their knees, praying it might be so
that as he boasts he is the Chosen One.
Aye, chosen for tragedy, memorable
as the worst and the most of the lost.

Inaugural

For what is my grief but a resolution?

My means is my sorrow.

Forever after—what actually is possible?

The free flight of crows to where and why unknown at dusk.

The ice-cramped rivulet, without a single word singing.

Can I refuse to desist?

Tears that have no answer.

Courage, yes, but must I make amends?

I was the boy on the bus.

To whom will I address my envelope of dreams?

I became the woman in a chemise.

You remember the office of horrors, correct?

Starfish under the sea—wasn't that what I believed?

In the dark behind me, those are children playing.

(January 20, 2017)

Here's What I Want, America

I want people thinking hard about such things as irony
and homophones, like entomology,
which has to do with insects and their instincts,
while etymology is words, their origins, and people
crossing borders, telling stories to each other.
I want a President at least as smart as the kid
who's flipping flap-jacks for a living wage,
a breast for every baby,
more pussy hats, and kittens in baskets adopted,
a bigger dick for anyone who thinks they really need one,
a temporary tat on my butt in gothic script
that reads *The living end*.
And I want poems composed with total concentration
for readers unafraid of deviations, off key verses
like I remember singing, *My country, tis of thee*,
one hot Sierra afternoon, swinging a hammer
building Jerry Tecklin's cabin, and swigging beer:
July 4th, 1976. Is it too late for another party?

Carry Me Back

In a narrow snowbound lane
on a slick road my dad and me
for Lincoln's birthday smack the Pontiac
suddenly before us: I bash the glass
before I realize what has happened,
hot blood splashing from my forehead.
I am almost eleven, barely in my body:
decades later and my brain behind the scar
still pulls me into the windshield of that car.

This is the year when much is stitched and much
remains undone, when I, a sturdy little boy,
get a first glimpse of my mortality.
My wound, a sutured gash
among the welts remaining
where a doctor, piece by painful piece,
plucked shards of shattered glass,
my wound sets me apart from other boys
—that, and wanting desperately to own a horse.

This is the year, 1961, when my favorite,
Carry Back—*the little brown colt*
from the wrong side of the tracks—
circles the pack to win the Derby.
While I mend, I watch as he, *The People's Choice*
nearly takes the Triple Crown. I grieve the loss.
I write to his owner, who writes back,
inviting me to meet my champion:
"Show this letter at the track."
The next summer, cleared by Pinkertons,
my dad and I are chauffeured
in a limousine at Saratoga,
saluted as we pass. My dad especially is thrilled;
no more of his regrets about my scar,

and this because, despite the odds,
my words won what I wanted.

At the stable, at an unmarked stall,
a guard absurdly calls the Derby winner "she"
and suddenly I doubt: can this be he?
My horse is lying on his side in straw;
when he stands, his gold flecked tail
trails nearly to the floor, and then I'm sure.
I turn around and here I am once more
going where I'm coming back: 1961.
An "upside down year," the last until 6009.

After Breakfast in Provincetown

Americans are so enamored of equality,
they would rather be equal in slavery than unequal in freedom.
—Alexis de Tocqueville

I feel as if I'm visiting from someplace far away,
from France, perhaps, or farther, yes—from Jupiter—
while drinking coffee, San Francisco Blend,
from a cup branded New England,
at the farthest eastern reach of America.

I'm hardly noticeable,
slouched dockside in a chair,
and under brilliant skies I disappear
where sleepy tourists queue to board
the Boston ferry and whale-watching boats.
It's peaceful here: none of that
corporate mob in black-glassed limousines,
and on the wet strand, but a few steps
from these seaside slips and planks,
no pirates to be seen.

Instead, somewhere behind me,
to the left, I suddenly hear de Tocqueville,
speaking of his visit when
observing our classless society
and nascent penal system,
he was so impressed.
        Cher Alexi, I address him,
my tone mildly corrective,
today we're not one nation under God,
and many, being self-righteous and unreflective
in the name of individualism,
deny the existence of Hell or the necessity
of repentance for their crimes,
but instead prize evasion of justice

more highly than any social contract.

Mon vieux,
        when you were last here,
you thought our prisons humane
and lauded their innovations
as you contemplated the responsibilities
you would need to assume back in France.
You must have wondered,
as I still do, what
this continent's wealth
requires of its conquerors.

Prescient as you were, could you have foreseen
that a hundred fifty years since then
our prisons would function less
to foster penitence and educate inmates
than to profit those who own them?

There's a saying that the Moon
is never so near as it appears.
Jupiter has dozens,
Metis being most dear to me,
she who's named for Jove's first wife,
an Oceanid, the goddess
of deep thought—

        Mon dieu,
how far from America I feel
while drinking my morning coffee
in the sun on MacMillan Pier!

1968

It wasn't all paisley, patchouli, and pot
that year—but I would graduate hopeful,

my follies quite harmless, and when
a group of us captured the flag and flew it

half-mast because Dr. King had been killed,
I felt solemn, bold, intelligent.

Bobby Kennedy was shot that summer—
there was much that was too much for words—

and some of us didn't make it into college
and were soon flying choppers into the jungle.

Some thought that love could change the world.
Then Chicago erupted: in the streets, kids were beaten,

and leaving for Europe, I was warned about Paris.
I got lost in Venice and missed getting laid,

but my girl was still waiting for me at home,
her breasts under gingham like peaches—

we weren't meant for more, and at Cornell
a farm boy no longer, I wrote stories

and poems, one about the calves
whose butchered parts I'd found in a field.

That year I learned about Nam:
a school chum on leave from the war,

a medic who'd handled the awful, told me
I'd never understand unless I was there.

Everybody Wants to Give Me their Woodstock

It's 50 years since and you'd think enough Woodstock
has been passed around to feed the hungry loaves and fishes,
to glean all the pearls from the mud, to make plenty merry
during the slow birth of Aquarius with his jars of honey and wine—
so, why must I bother when opening a journal to any
unknown photo scan the blurry faces for my own
on the fabled hillside, or in some line of brothers and sisters
clambering through muck at dawn back to sleep
in the Galaxie 500 I'd driven to Bethel with my buddy?
Because of the dream, I reply, looking over yet another
image in of all places The London Review of Books—
because of that recurring dream of the young, who don't know
better than to imagine a better world, one more free, more sane—
because of the way that great dope—*fuck, yeah*—shocked me
to see that what I'd thought true was only what I thought,
and not the Tree of Life, *the other tree*, in the Garden, the one
whose fruit is immortality, which was my intimation
while once listening to Garcia's guitar, each note independent
of what had come before or might come after, but also
perceiving how all of them, moving through time, were free of it—
because of the music, man—the music at the festival, which was,
like they say, only as good as what any of us was happening.

1984

That was when I first heard God.
Back then, it was always unannounced
and could happen anywhere—the graveyard
next to S.U.N.Y. was my favorite
—I went to God plenty of times.
When Reagan was reelected, of course,
in that snowstorm: God was really good that night.
It was the big band with hand-drummers
and the Devil-May-Care singers,
three black girls and three white for backup,
and two fat guys playing tambourines.
Forgive me, but that's how we talked back then.
Nowadays God won't allow it, everything has to be vetted
and God's lawyers are serious about this,
though I'm allowed to say how good the music
always was and will always be. Everybody knows
about the choirs of angels, and you've seen
the paintings of Fra Angelico, how beautiful
their horns and harps of gold and tongues of flame—
but, hey, God has never even needed a microphone!
Angels are optional. And today the Street Kids, they have
their own scene with wild dance styles and all.
But God—Holy Geeze—God is still outta sight!

Lies, All Lies

—after Stanley Kunitz

A poet is a lyre,
but so what?

Metaphors, metaphors. . .

Some say that you couldn't take the truth.
Some say they'd be better off dead.
Others say they only want to live without fear,
and to some, that sounds like a lie.

If it sounds like a lie, then. . .

If you believe everything you hear, then. . .

If seeing is believing, then
you need to get your eyes examined—
though some say you can't ever trust the doctors.
There are those who die every way imaginable,
for example, right now in Syria and Yemen,
but what's that to you?

The truth is whatever I say is the truth, say some
so decisively you almost could trust them.

Why not stop resisting,
the evidence doesn't lie, but
is it the whole story?
Sometimes the opposite could also be true.

Some say we were born to love,
but others claim that it's to cry,
or, say some, to do better than this.

Sometimes the meaning of a text
is in the subtext, and it can
call into question where
you thought you were headed.

Are you still with me?
Do you believe the truth is like candy?
Or is it an apple, an orange,
the color chartreuse?

If four horses drink from a stream,
one pinto, one palomino,
a strawberry roan, and a bay-brown,

how would you choose
which to ride into town?

Corona Crisis Search Results

This morning at my screen I scroll in hopes
of finding news that our pandemic will conclude,

news of a new vaccine or treatment, or that
perhaps the genome of the virus has a fatal flaw,

and despite its urge for replication,
its mutations will result in its extermination.

There's nothing I can do about the fools
who mask themselves from common sense

in their god's name, or in defiance of community.
Do politicians count as vectors of the virus?

I'm not alone in searching facts about the Plague
that helped to end the Middle Ages—

did survivors think the victims had no choice
but follow Death? Images of *La Danse Macabre*

portray a grinning skeleton with whom the living
link their hands—yet often they look gay!

Death's an echo of the newborn's cry.
Do toddlers sense they're in a roundelay?

Some doctors tout a thing that I have always done:
dancing with abandon to music that I love.

Madison Square Garden, 1939

—after A Night at the Garden by Marshall Curry

White nationalist rally, 20,000, viewed online one recent rain-
    soaked afternoon—

"What could happen here has happened here," I wrote, as
    baleful music played, my fingers moving on my keyboard.

Why are we so easily misled by crowing crackpots?

Why assent in mindless unison when someone tells a mob
    exactly what they're told they want to hear?

Sunshine broke the clotted sky. I proceeded then, *adagio,*

like a child on a crowded street searching for his parent's hand
    amid a crowd of strangers,

searching headlines on the Web: no fool or tyrant had so far
    undone the world.

Headwinds shifted; trees outside my window showered yellow
    leaves, *allegro ma non troppo.*

Sixties, the Sixties

It was more than ten years of superglue and politics.

*

The world is sunshine when we're young.

*

Golden or gaunt, naive, amoral or sheltered,
children can ignore the fact that overhead

treetops snap in ravaging winds—and how
the storm, this storm, that storm is always rising.

*

We're old enough to stop
embellishing the decade.

*

The scent of pine duff is a reassurance—
soon enough, I'll be underground

and maybe will emerge another kind of man,
a kinder man perhaps. Or come back female.

*

Her too, him too, them too, us too, you too
will likely someday weep about your revolutions.

Last night returned me Uncle Wiggily,
a rabbit on a child's game board—and instantly
Salinger's tale of two women lost in Connecticut.

*

Soldiers dead for fifty years appear to me.

*

Music claiming love is all we need
can tear me from my grief and rage.

Astonished

Let it be known there is a fountain
That was not made by the hands of men
—Robert Hunter

I'll tell you what astonishes me:
at 5:52 a.m. it's still dark and the temp
is minus ten Fahrenheit,
and I'm astonished as I write this,
that Robert Hunter is,
although present in my mind,
absent—absent but also present.
Just moments ago in a dream
I was backing a large SUV
out of a tight parking spot,
and then he was in my living room
singing "Ripple," intoning it strangely,
seeming to panic when
he couldn't remember a word:
I piped up, "music," when actually,
as I knew immediately upon waking,
the line is *Let there be songs to fill the air.*
Then I remembered Hunter is dead.

Outside my window, it's so black
that I can see my face clearly
on the glass in a darkness
inseparable from the reflection.
I'm astonished that writing this,
Cairo suddenly comes to mind,
the time that a hustler promised
my wife and me that if we ate pigeon meat
at his brother's café down the street,
we could make love all night long.
Cairo, near to me this morning
but also very far away—Cairo,

where the Great Sphinx lives in Giza,
across the street from Nazlet El-Semman.

The world's largest sculpture,
a lion-man, carved from the plateau's bedrock,
where for thousands of years
it's been watching the sky for when
the star-shape of Leo will rise again
on the horizon, as it did
around 25,000 years ago.
The builders seem to have known
that we, who nowadays sift
subatomic particles searching for God,
would need to be reminded
of the order in the sky, and what's
behind it. Astonishing.
By the way, Kaphre didn't have the statue made,
and Thutmose only restored it: the Sphinx
seems always to have been there
like a great cat crouching.
I'm astonished all of this makes sense to me
as I contemplate my reflection
in a window so black I'm once again
back in Egypt, the Black Land—
no, actually this doesn't astonish me,
although it is quite amazing how every morning
out of dreams and memories I'm recreated.

Good Morning America (courtesy ABC, 9/29/05)

Deadly flu inevitable, only Swiss company Roche makes cure,
      no nation owns enough when, not if, pandemic strikes,
      don't ask why US never stockpiled, start now, 60 people
      dead world-wide, bird danger wakeup call.

Also, President's approval rating never lower as House Hammer
      DeLay indicted claims innocence of money laundering.
      "No daylight" between the two says source, while
      news pundits declare scandal spin must top speed
      handle many woes, even Senator Frist big heart-doc
      contender for oval office getting stock deals scrutinized,
      and don't forget gasoline is short, expensive, don't
      forget hurricanes mismanaged, Iraqi war news daily
      worsening, and Cheney's staff chief Libby finally admits
      he leaked secret agent's name, remember?

Now monster mold threatens New Orleans. Ugly stench
      doctor's home, he wears surgical mask and latex gloves live
      amid fuzzy grime that circles parlor walls, coats picture
      frames, water line like river wharf splotchy black yuck.
      Fascinating. "This is still a good place to live!" hopeful guy
      declares. And from New York City studio Diane Sawyer
      reminds viewers round the planet—me in Qatar watching
      wide-eyed—these homes will all be demolished.

Being blond helps in on-line dating, results study 30,000 on-line
      daters, valuable as college degree in these circles
      polltakers conclude.

Then there's the giant squid, white, long as a building is tall,
      photographed 20,000 leagues under the sea by Japanese,
      head guy smiling like a kid displays long tentacle
      accidentally nabbed can still suck with suction cups his
      fingers—"So strange feeling!" Used squid as bait.

Pray these stories don't escape their box, please pray peace on
      Earth, salaam, shalom is not just super-marketeering
      what you need to buy or else things only get worse—
      truth to say the TV never answers me when I pray.

Still, here's superstar George Clooney recovering torn dura
      mater membrane of spinal cord, exercising wit in Italian
      villa personal tour for Ms. Sawyer who gah-gah gushes
      "A guy from Kentucky has a pizza room!" New movie
      he directed about Edward R. Murrow nemesis Senator
      McCarthy inquisitions title *Good Night, and Good Luck*,
      was signature of newsman's newsman—used years ago
      in a poem of mine, I'd just like to mention—Clooney,
      very classy, won't take bait about girlfriend preference
      blond or brunette, looks happy being himself, average
      Joe who's who.

On the Wet Wide Air

You could see it was raining, the rain, it kept falling.
You could tell the rain, rain, you could tell it, stop
and it didn't—but sometimes it did what you said.
Then, after dark last night the fire flies arrived.
Some of them burning so bright they left trails
on the wet wide air: little rockets.
Fairy-like. Insect intelligent mysterious lights.

My Body, Your Body

Our bodies like matchsticks,
our bodies like smoke,
like wood dappled with flames,
our bodies like yellowing leaves,
our bodies like broken glass,
our bodies like strings of rain,
like flowers exploding with seeds,
like torrents of rain,
our bodies never the same
after love, our bodies
all the same
quite gone after death.

Our bodies alive with hope,
our bodies also of hate,
our possessive bodies,
our bodies afraid to grow old,
our bodies like tumblers of brandy,
our bodies like chalices of gold,
our bodies like rainbows,
our bodies of light made to shimmer,
our bodies arrayed with the stars,
our bodies of galactic proportions,
our bodies like baskets of blood,
our bodies of loam, of mud,
our bodies on loan from the sun,
our bodies,
our bodies.

Where do we keep their true hearts?
Is the soul to be found
among nerves, in synapses
sparkling with joy, crackling
with horror at the cruelties
our bodies inflict on each other?

Where are the mothers, the fathers
with kisses like bread for their children?
Where, right now, is my own body
whose breath is this song,
whose questions so vital?

Why are we killed in the name of a god?
Why are we traded for pieces of silver?
Why do some bodies burn,
why are some bodies faceless,
why do the eyes of so many go blank,
their voices gone dumb
while their digits are twiddling keys,
and outside their doors
the bodies of others lie dead?
Somebody answer me now:
I require your answer in person!

I insist that your body,
human as mine,
be humble as salt
and bold as a diamond at dawn,
gracious as corn,
erotic as an orchid,
and proud as a tower of wheat.
Your body, my body
soft as the down of a gosling,
fierce as a falcon falling from heaven,
silent as water under the grass,
smooth as the skin on warm milk,
bright as the tongue of a cat.

Void of desire,
or craven, or cold,
brimming with passion,

detached or self-sacrificing,
ignorant, eloquent, jealous, divine—
our bodies soon gone.

Our bodies, the bodies
we dance through.

Suffer the Little Children

This is what Jesus said, according to the Gospels
of_____.

To suffer is painful, but means also to admit, and children,
despite or because of their innocence_____.

He also said, "for the kingdom of God belongs
to_____."

Jesus, say Christians, is God, the Son of God, whose love saves
the world, and He is also called the Son of _____.

In fulfillment of a prophecy, and just like anyone of woman
born, Jesus had to _____.

But the story continues: He came back in order
to_____.

If you believe all this, then you
must_____.

Whether or not you believe, the pain, the misery of those
who want, as we all do, to live happily _____.

The First Stone

they deserve to be hated
and yet I don't want to—

murderers—

I could hate them
but won't—

they need to be
renounced and I do
I do, of course—

they should be
caught and punished
and maybe even killed—

pain isn't like a stone
in a stream
worn away by time—

there is no stone to throw
where my sorrows
can't be drowned—

I want to hate them
but won't, and don't
and don't know how
to stop them—

give me the stone
that can't be thrown.

Weird Weather

I shall walk naked hither and yon,
raising my voice

waking the stones
to their nature:

when the winds tumble
down the silver buds

and rivers roar approval,
I shall rejoice

with the order of clouds—
see, I am taken,

see, I am shaken
to my bones

yet the hail
hurteth me not,

for the lightning
is my tongue.

I thunder the sky,
and with stars I prophesy:

flood, fire, and landslide.
Let the leaders beware—

I shall wake the stones
to their nature.

For I am the bull of heaven
and the heifer he mounts.

I, the good woman
suave in my skin.

I, the man whose rod
of a snake is made.

On Hearing that Bob Creeley Died

I left the party where I,
a prize winner, ought to have
been networking the worth
of my book like everyone else,
but instead, seeing you about
to split for a smoke
I joined you, Bob—the last time
we hung out. I don't tell this story
to puff me up or praise you
for your cool, but for poetry,
how we stepped into an April night,
Gramercy Park blooming,
forsythia under misty rain.
I've often thought since then
This is the life of poets,
and to remember you,
this is what I've got.

World Headquarters: Late March

1.
In this vacancy I have lately acquired
        a means to delight
                in sensible objects, and if you could
                    would you see,
                look anyway
        into my head and out my eyes—then again
I myself do not consider my mind
        to be lodged cranially, and if
its nature is devoid of definition,
        then more importantly
                all of this that occupies my attention

is for what purpose?

When, as if a ram in a thicket, I believed myself
        at the center of things,
                myself, my mind, or what—
the world headquarters—
        I was among bare trees

whose twig tips, scribbling on the sky
        revealed the emptiness to which I refer—
no object, no subject—
        no obstacle—

this came to me:
                all these trees want
        is to *tree*.

See how they spread themselves upwardly,
        swaying and creaking,
voicing the bare sky in late March;
        they do not wait to leaf,

have not a thought for their immanent buds:
                    they do not lack, but have grace
and strength more than enough
            to stand before the wind
and all else demanding that they change.

2.
"All intelligence is artificial,"
            a polymath once proclaimed to me.
The bughouse—I remember his fondness for it,
as if for a home away from home:
            orbited by loving caretakers, he
reciprocated as a star does
            with its steady emission of light
all that embraced him maternally.

We are indeed star stuff, congealed quanta of info,
            brain waves and particles of decision, etc.,
                        and mostly ignorant
that we live within our own star's heliosphere.
I ask myself why I am prone to
            linguistic excess, since nothing of import
                        can be explained that already

is not experienced—why,
            when observing some naked trees
                        I allude to that vacancy amid their upraised limbs
                        and the sky they seem to touch

as a means by which to speak of the space any figure
            occupies: every single thing

interdependent with its surroundings,
            is interpenetrated by the same space,
whose nature can't be grasped

—hence, this also my sage friend said:
        facts are not made but uncovered.

3.
To the trees once more, who dance in unison,
        who sing the March wind
               up into their branches:
               see where their limbs are entwined
        unthinkingly like lovers?

Among our kind, simply holding hands
               is proven to alleviate pain,
        and to graze the body of another
can induce ecstasy.
                      Regard your own fingers
        branching as mine do on this page
where I inscribe these words,
        on this desktop stained with the prints of time,
its wooden surface planed smooth,
        perhaps a hundred years ago
               a living tree:
what is the reach of your identity?
Touch, like sight, is photons
        streaming from our sun to us
and streaming through:
        we are this stuff gloriously,
and all flesh being grass,
therefore,
        photosynthetically

—so say the fire cherry trees,
where they hold themselves
        black and bare,
               wind-tossed on the depthless blue.

Simple Dissolution

Here's how it will be: simple dissolution
like droplets of fog drifting further apart
according to the third law of thermodynamics
always at odds with what holds
the Whole Shebang together, gravity
or whatever we puny humans believe.
The Big Deal will continue without us,
but it will seem that what once was
constant is now only memory,
and all that made sense will be dismissed
like so much piffle falling from the sky.
There will be no heaven or hell,
and the money that bound them
will be worthless at the End.
Some will be dissipated, non compos mentis,
feet aching from treks to the mountains,
to the seashore, hikes to find
candy stores recalled from childhood,
and all of this will seem like a dream, and so
we'll keep asking each other, *Is this a dream?*
Can this really be happening?
And then we'll be ready for the Next:
it won't arrive in starships
to harvest us like stalks of wheat,
threshing the grain from the chaff: the Next
will barely be noticeable, because in fact it will have
already begun, ignored while we were frantic
about losing the Last, that beautiful thing
dissolving before our eyes, that golden mist
woven of sunlight and water.
How sad people will be as it escapes their grasp!
A few, hoping to sound wise or at least resigned,
will say, *It was all we ever really needed,*
and we wasted our chances to save it!

You and I won't have to bother to take notes
like Pliny the Elder observing
the death of Pompeii under scalding ash,
since our history will be irrelevant
to the denizens of the Next World,
who will have their own mortality to face
and errors to make if they are human as we,
imperfect, but worthy of love.
Will they ask themselves if what appears to be
the End isn't only the universe exhaling,
blowing itself open so that it can
breathe itself in once again,
or will they believe that myth matters not?
I think it might also be a kind of liberation
but only if we aren't stuck on the thought
it wasn't supposed to happen like this.

II

ad-Dawḥa

The Peninsula

On this gypsum spur you learn to compromise.
Dust filled skies, high winds, sun glowering:
a fleet of *dhows* waiting out a sandstorm.

Meanwhile, gas beneath the desert floor wells up
and into bank accounts, colossal wealth accrues:
"We count in billions." Off shore, there's more.

Once you were a desert people, camels packing
few possessions to the outskirts of the Rub al-Khali.
On your isthmus, *ad-Dawha* became a fishing town.

Bismillah—in the name of God—you still give
your daughters. Some for pride betroth the bride,
but others—lucky ladies, I was told—are they

whose white-robed grooms arrive with love
besides abundant *mahr*. Four wives are still allowed
but nowadays expensive to keep happy.

Every path recedes behind a journey.
Now, your women drive themselves in black Mercedes.
The culture of your children grows a mystery.

World Lit

> *My soul has grown deep like the rivers.*
> —Langston Hughes

We were in the southern Sahara, not too far
across the sea from India, reading in English
Langston Hughes, a favorite of my students:
"The Negro Speaks of Rivers."
How old is older than human blood? I asked.
And the rivers—what's older than their water?

*

I tried to teach them many things besides
the language they would need in med school.
My country's history began with genocide,
I once said, and progressed because of slavery,
and we're proud of what our Founders
preached but didn't truly practice.
Fatima told me she had spent a year in a school
in Colorado. The name from Spanish
means *colored red,* a reference to the sandstone
rather than the natives. A beautiful state, she said.
Did you unveil your face, and taste our freedoms?
Both, she replied, although in Qatar
she once again was covered.

*

One day I said, It's likely all of us have ancestors
who traded slaves or were enslaved.
To the Romans, these were *servus* and *serva.*
Andrei pointed out the word in English
comes from *Slavs*, those whose languages are Slavic.
Sclava is Latin and recalls a woman
taken captive—*schiava* in Italian.
Till today Schiavone is a surname
widely found: it's from Old Venetian

for those taken from Dalmatia.
By the way, Rome wasn't built in a day—
it was built by slaves.

*

My surname, fairly common in Naples
and the region of Campania marks me as
a lucky one. Was my ancestor among those
who escaped Vesuvius in A.D. 79?
Or is my family descended from freed slaves
in Rome—maybe the very gladiator whose name
is graffitied on the Coliseum's wall?

*

I tried to teach them how to test the value
of opinions; I tried to cultivate their sense of taste.
With acquired words and new ideas,
with searching eyes they sought to know what's true.
I said I most respect submission to the order
that a person finds and follows from within.
I paraphrased Chuang-Tzu. He knew
the joy of fishes playing in a river—
walking near that water, he was joyful too.

Capital Q

1.
Lately, while I'm making English come alive in Qatar,
lately I've been telling students of my life back home.

By the way, it's not pronounced like *Gutter*—as Bush Junior did—
but in English more like *Cutter.* Where I'm living all alone.

2.
I used to be a typesetter, taking pleasure
in the heft of letters, words and sentences inverted

and reversed in my composing stick. So I know
the *miniscule,* or lower case, do most all the heavy lifting.

The *majuscule,* like upper classes everywhere, have got it easy—
except for Q: the capital has little u to carry on its tail.

3.
"Cue you," I might say, pointing to myself in a mirror
as if directing a scene from my life. Reversed

I could be *A man of questionable character*—I'm not,
but sometimes feel the part, cut off from my wife

in Doha. Here, family rhymes with life, and bachelors
like lonely lions are regarded warily. Or else pitied.

White collar and tie at work, my residence a spacious flat,
still I'm one of many paid to do the country's heavy lifting.

When students ask me how I manage all alone, I quote
my house cleaner: "Oh, sir, you must be strong!"

La Forza

Although I no longer care to shatter the looking glass
so vivid in my recollection—floor length, its silver
backing that we kids believed was mercury, spider-

cracked, pocked, and weird with black eyeballs
where we'd shot with BBs to break its spell—
and though tonight I've thought myself a know-it-all,

Professor Pot with a dented lid who likes to clang about,
I've always been a cook who delights in feeding other people.
In the black window of my flat, I see the fellow

looking back at me, twenty stories high, backed
by the nascent city's silver lights—buildings
incomplete, always reaching—and almost think

I could be living on a San Francisco hilltop,
be an actor in a film, a guy possessed of *la forza*—
fortitude—someone handy to have around,

his needs shaved to a rind of cheese, a heel of bread,
and not the hungry fool I've seen myself today.
But I haven't come this far to make a fiction of my life.

Words Before Dawn

Night loud and no respite—
the gap between sleep and wakefulness.

Construction as promised;
erratic metallic noise breaking through.

Visions must be kept burning, it's true,
fueled with intention, exactingly surveyed

made manifest with capital on demand.
Where I step back into my dream

black chaos is ordered in an age of iron,
the future summoned vertically.

Al Shaqab
                    for Marco Ameduri

This is the desert of shoveled sand,
heaps of rubble-rock,
grinding machines,
                    its lost peace promised
for a future along avenues of light
when date-palms will be planted
where nothing much can grow
unless men make it so.

                    A desolate night,
yet haloed with dust and dim stars
a full moon outshines the work-lights
on tractors who roar like the sea
against the sand
                    as we prowl in our car
past the walls of our old riding school
defunct in the name of progress.

Yet the breeding farm still stands:
here and there a stable hand
notes our passage, but says nothing:
we are white after all, and maybe important,
so blatant are we, moving among the horses.
Three mares in their paddock
amble toward us to be touched,
and across a sand-swallowed track,
solitary where he's penned
a gray stallion trots near,
neck curved like a crescent moon,
nose that could fit into a teacup:
he has rubbed his face raw
through the rails for them.

It's in his blood, I tell my friend,
despite all this—
                    waving my hand
past the dozers and diggers
tearing open the night—

he knows what the moonlight is for.

Impossible Dream

Behind me black smoke twisting on the empty sky.

Battle pennants, blood-red streamers in the streets.

Bales of money—riyals, dirhams, dollars, euros—pixels that pile
around decimal points, disappear from plasma screens
and fly up the noses of memory sticks.

Smiling men who snort seriously.

Women who balance on hard heels.

The price per barrel and what will the market support.

Behind me a forest falls—*hush, darling, nobody hears.*
White water stalls behind dams: the blank faces of power.

"I could tell you stories about this business."

Geiger counter scratching loudly through my sleep.

A hill of fire.

Wind from the north.

In the valley, they tremble and choke,
down where a mine crumbled last week.

Cheap subsidies.

"Char-broiled—what do you call them—*bonuses.*"

Electing the night because sunlight hurts their eyes,
the children in terminal beds, boy soldier amputees,
their mothers who turn tricks.

Who's got a better reason?

"Say, friend, is that Jack or Jim in your glass?"

Behind me the scabs and swollen walls,
lovers who praise God with heavy tongues.

I'm afraid of falling under titanium cleats,
what with the price of gold and everybody climbing.

My back aches, shoulder points stab,
the lymph in my armpits begins to freeze,
pecker retracts despite the prospect of a summit—
and then waking from this dream, I'm still asleep.

Angry eyes, bulbous nose and thick mustache,
inches from my face, accusing me,
taut lips, growling, "What about our families?"

Chew me like chicken, gnash my bones to splinters,
spit me into the sand for the lizards and rats.

All of this behind me.

Black smoke twisting free, tall stacks
flaring off impurities.

Praise for the Workers of Doha

Eating melon from the tip of a long knife
behind broad glass, looking over the city
from my air conditioned flat.

Outside, the loud *clang* of a work gang
once more at dawn, a swarm
of anonymous men, dark skinned,
blue clad, hard hatted,
wearing masks and neckerchiefs
against the desert sun

high in the frame of a tower
among many towers
rising around me on the white plain.

They swing their yellow crane
hoisting tubes of scaffolding
and bundles of rebar.

They bend, squat, lift, cut carefully,
and tie an iron lattice, a skeletal deck
they daily and nightly tread.

Whack, whack, they nail together
wooden boards, and soon
they'll pump cement up
from a mixer-truck
to fill these forms,
and then repeat the cycle,
layering slabs of concrete
story after story.

What ease at such height in such heat!

I am cool and almost chilled,
my melon sweet, taking care with my knife
and my words not to slip.

All Souls Day

Northern light.
Heaps of clouds.
My mother in my thoughts.
            *

Bedroom closet,
my wife's blouse
inherited from mom—
polyester print in pink and sepia,
sheer, silk-like, cheaply made—
frugal mamma.
            *

Wife whose empty clothing hangs
in my apartment, wife who's
seven thousand miles back at home.
            *

Days of the Dead.
Rumbling town at working dawn.
Desert winter waiting rain.
Cool nights when I can feel alive.
            *

Men in *thobes* all white,
women cloaked in black *abaya*
at the *souk* where I ate fish
and bought a block of resin
for the strings of my *rababah.*
Goat skin box, horsehair bow
to play my *Bedu* blues.

(Doha, Qatar, 2/11/2008)

Figures of Speech

Give me a cave to meditate, a fire,
one star burning brightest, and a tribe

to follow, rising every night and falling,
tales I might recall. Let me see them

clothed in immortality.
Let each give me its light, light

that looks unending. But give me too
the scent of human labor—don't disguise it.

War is a curse to be broken. Our songs
exceed our exile to a stony place.

Business Class

You might think the Earth had been flattened,
unrolled like a map and delivered to you,
looking down while you fly in Business Class.

You might think you've joined a group
of global masters, rather than become
a type of drone controlled from down below.

You're comfortable with the whisky in your glass,
and though you're not so pampered as
the customers in First, does anyone aboard believe

that when they land they'll be exempt from gravity?
A bit of Einstein you recall predicts that if a rocket
were to travel far enough in outer space,

when slingshot back to where it started, time aloft
would have passed at quite a different rate
than back on Earth. The loved ones which the crew

had counted on returning to, would have
long before been dust. The weight of such a loss
unthinkable, you take a sip and shift attention

to the screen before you: altitude is 37,000 feet
above Iraq. You slide to a window and stare
at the Tigris and Euphrates rivers,

at Mesopotamia in the orange dusk.
Long straight waterways, long empty roads.
An eerie calm, perhaps the aftermath

of another misbegotten battle.
Drawing near, a flight attendant asks,
"What's happening down there?"

"They're having a war," you answer.
She takes one look, resumes her post,
then offers you another drink.

Samarasa, the Flavor of Equanimity

—homage to Denise Levertov

Where mind moves,
it also is unmoving—

And the beggar boy in Peshawar
has the legs of the kid in Miami

And when the cattle of Kobe are fed
the goats in Ryanggang fatten

The water of Dakar
is the water of New York

My mosquitos
are your mosquitos

My apple, bite by bite consumed
is that of the guy in Doha

And the homosexuals of Uganda
are equal to those of Poughkeepsie

And the dead of L.A.
are dead as the dead of Manila

If this is the taste of wisdom,
then this is how wisdom tastes—

empty of distinctions,
void of substance—

now what about that beggar boy
in Peshawar?

Surrender the World

Okay, maybe you fight
for your bread: you could quit.
Got children? Get smart.
If you don't love, you lose.
Nobody told you?

The whole world knows
it's going no place.
Hum along if you like.
Even if you like it,
bird song doesn't last.

Why not neglect to name
everything bad
three times a day?
Independence
isn't rocket science,
red glare, dividends.

Save the day, hero,
accomplish nothing—
what the birds say
sitting in the tippy-tops
at dawn.

At the Inland Sea, Khawr al Udayd

Ali's tea is "My tea," brewed special
for our caravan of execs, locals, expats,
plus one Turkish dignitary, plus me,
the friend of a friend invited along for my poetry.

Wandering about in his heavy robe,
prepared already for the nighttime cold,
headlamp strapped to his brown brow,
giant teapot in his hands, again and again he calls,
"Who wants my tea? None like it anywhere!"

With milk and sugar, spiced secretly —
trace of cinnamon, cardamom, buds of clove?—
boiled up in his cauldron, it's no ordinary *karak chai*
he serves cocoa-colored in glass mugs.

"Your tea is mighty," I say.
"My tea is your tea," I jest.

Tents on the sea shore, stars overhead, by fire light
Nezar plays guitar, sings like Eric Clapton:
"You look wonderful tonight…"

Amina teaches me to clap along
to Arab songs like in Morocco.
Essa's oud keeps ringing even when
at last I'm in my sleeping bag.

Next morning: breakfast fire, water boiling,
sun shining, dew drying, people yawning.
"Did we sing last night? Did we dream?"
Now let the party begin again,
let these final precious moments count.

Ali goes swimming, floats on his back
in the warm buoyant water,
sips a glass of his famous brew:
"Look, look, I'm drinking my tea in the sea!"

Essa strums his oud and I begin to improvise a poem:
Hello and goodbye to newfound friends,
the sweet and salty taste of this.

Later, breaking camp, "Remember my tea!"
that madman calls to me.

No Foot, No Horse

The right front tire of my rented Lancer is low;
not exactly flat, but plump and healthy it is not,
leaking, leaking how long I don't know.

On Doha's C Ring Road I leave The Rider
where I've bought a pair of spurs, and trust
that I can manage back to Al Markhiya station
on my way to teach at Weill Cornell—

game, albeit lame, that is, cavalier.

*

Horsepower: we think of engines.
Opening the hood like looking in a mouth
to reckon length and wear of tooth.

Kicking tires like we lift their feet
to study hooves, the health of frogs and bulbs.

Jammed in traffic, just ahead of me a stallion rears—
that is, the icon on a red machine
whose style speaks Italian.
Farriers were surely at the foot of all that fame:
Ferrari is a smithy by another name.

*

Mahn, he's called, the groom who tacks my mount.
A Nepali packing sacks of bedding, mucking stalls
and proudly rubbing leather clean
for six expensive horses.

Once I took his hand to thank him,
felt it crusted, cracked and something like a hoof.

Today he whispers to me as he works, bent over
fitting boots to my mount's feet:
"Doctor horses? Doctor people?"

I know what's coming when he opens his raw palms
and fumbles words about the pain.

Hedyah

Old mare, mother, *mère, à la mer*—
at the sea, on the beach—dying—on the sand
a scarlet plume trailing from your vulva,
"bleeding frankly" a doctor would say,
while we watch, waiting for word
to the vet on her mobile, waiting for consent
for euthanasia—we gather in the shadow
of the van, being human with you,
helping you in any way we can, toweling
cool water over your neck and flanks,
holding your head, as you fail again
to find your feet, old mother, flailing
your hooves on the packed sand, gasping
to stand, your long horse face, grandmother,
facing heaven—28 year Arabian gray,
how many foals did you drop on this land,
uterus now prolapsed, extruding
raw and red as if itself to be born at last—
and now your death arrives,
now the vet has heard, and she injects first
a large milky dose to kill your pain,
punching right into the jugular vein,
and a moment later through the same IV
shoots you full of death, delivers you peace,
Hedyah, whose name means Gift,
and we who will grieve you
are grateful you lived.

Arabians

If a horse's shadow
is big as the horse
but weighs as much
as nothing—
then what of the body
made of light?

*

A draft horse draws.
A light horse drums.

*

Gallop: to run.
The horse with its feet
hitting three beats
flies with all four in the air.

*

The effortless wind, the sun.

*

Can you believe a man
who puts his face
into your hands
isn't asking for sugar
but for love?

*

Love is light,
made of light,
love is a name
for the light.

*

We rolled in the hay,
we prickled with pleasure.
At dawn, strolled the beach
where migrant flamingos
were wading.

*

Near Zakreet at a wadi
feral ostriches
fourteen hands high
strutted and hissed—
ride at your own risk!

*

My stallion Saleem,
once a marathon racer,
at Sheik Faisal's club
was overlooked:
another stud, another gray,
beautiful but ill mannered,
was bred instead
to the blue-ribbon mare.

*

Al Borak was given
by Gabriel
to Mohammed
to fly in the night
to Jerusalem:
The Lightning.

*

I jumped into the sun—
blinded, but my mount
Kasmir was wise
and leapt rightly.

*

We wore *thobes, guttras, aghals,*
our horses in decorative blankets
and braided rope bridles:
acting for a film about war.

We battled with swords
playing at war,
making a movie
that ended with love.

The Decent Thing to Do

In a country where decency can feel policed,
in a room where an important debate is to be filmed
and later broadcast on international TV,
here where experts soon will argue about a war—
or is it peace for Palestine they will be deciding—
in Doha, where tempting glances and witty banter
must respect sharia, I'm a guest. And here
right now, she's climbing up the stairs
looking at the empty chair beside me.

I take her measure with a furtive glance:
mid-calf skirt that's filigreed with gold,
hem that's lifting slightly
step by step as she approaches,
knees that step by step appear.
When I'm asked, as calmly as can be,
I say, "Please take the seat beside me."

She's just returned from holiday.
Australian, single mom, administrator
at a college near my own in Education City.
I want to touch her sun-touched hair,
and wish I'd been there basking with her
on a beach where no one else would stare.
We're flirting, and despite the talk of war,
at the moment, neither she nor I could care.
When a camera pans the audience,
in a monitor I spy our dalliance.
And then I see her see the wedding band on me.

Ten years later, I remember choosing to resist.
Ten years later, and in Palestine, their grief persists.

To Allen Ginsberg

Shafts of sunlight stenciling a pattern
of crosses through window sashes:
twentieth story, dawn light meeting
several posted color pages, downloads
of Blake's *Songs*, the two called "Nurse's Song"—
Oh, yes, night's cold dews fall soon, children.

Watching how the source of life plays on my wall,
watching as I write, hearing you read, Allen,
Ah, sunflower weary of time, a shadow draws past my eyes—
and yet, for the span of this letter, my pen is quick
my phantom friend, the morning stays.

Women's Work

An effort, this: the paring off of cherry flesh,
the plucking out of stones.

Ripe, too ripe wrapped tight in cellophane,
I saw the lattice of white mold

upon too many of the bright, black cherries
on their tray of Styrofoam, even as my mouth

began to water. Took up the sharpened blade
and sitting at my table, plates and bowls

before me, TV tuned to PM entertainment,
cut and cut, and watched the juices flow.

My fingers stained like henna: thought
of how the chic, cloaked women of this town

will sometimes flourish hands completely
laced with red-brown dye. *Mehndi*

is a ladies' art: a man would never wear it.
In India, a bride whose palms and wrists

have been so decorated doesn't work
for several days about the house. Then,

like me, she might well choose
the sharpest knife to whittle sweet

away from rotten meat, to cut the seed
out from the core. Or else a kitchen maid

will do the chore. That's who I am right now.
Master of these changes, master of my house.

Ya, Doha, Ya Doha

1.
Won't be lonely all my life—
but meanwhile I watch porn on satellite TV.
Wish my hard-core fantasy,
that one from Germany
were here in sheer black silk:
I'd buy her high-end perfume
at a desert diamond mall,
and we'd eat *shawarma*
just across the street.

2.
City Center: everybody passes through
and sidewise watches you
while stocking up on fancies.

I lean back, eyes closed, to rest my back
against a pillar just outside Carrefour.
I run my hand behind, around
the column's cool white surface,
jump awake when I am touched:

she's several steps behind her man
in *niqab* and *abaya*—I see nothing
but her probing eyes
that finding mine, shift off.

3.
Sometimes I'm the desert hermit
whose temptation breeds his meditation
from a less than perfect past.

Sometimes I am graced.

About to leave that shopping place,
heading downward on a moving stair
I have the sense of being watched:
an angel moving upward on the Jacob's Ladder
scrutinizes me, and through a veil
that's sheer as shadow—
almost like a bridal veil—
I gaze upon her almost hidden face.

Doha Ma'alsalaama

1.
Bang, bang! An oblivious crew
anonymous in baby blue overalls

wakes me from sleep with their hammers
stripping forms from concrete walls—

I struggle to wish peace and quiet for us all—
and suddenly a giant yellow crane

swings silently the heavy frames

away through sun-shot dusty air.

2.
City that was never mine, goodbye.
Blessings on your squads of workers

your molested housemaids, all-night drivers,
company tea boys old as grandpas.

Goodbye to your *thobes* and *gutras*,
to your chic *abayas* and Manolo Blahnik heels.

Beloved students, colleagues: will we meet again?
Flamingoes floating just off shore,

memories of horseback riding beachfront dawns,
sand mouse with your shadow

leaping from my mare's quick hooves

beyond the noisy nights and days remain.

3.
I learned my poems by heart, tried not to take so hard
Doha's constant racket—*acka, acka, ack*—rock-hammers

cracking limestone for the basements of towers:
I asked the locals, "Does the digging stir the djinn?"

I sickened often, breathing dust and flared off gases,
products of the country's new prosperity,

and learned to sleep with wax plugs in my ears.
One night I dreamt my absent wife seduced me

in the shade of maple trees back home.
"Here's your Aphrodite," she declared,

"your Amira—that's the name they call me here."
I woke alone with virus chill, with a dose

of William Blake consoling me:

Roses are planted where thorns grow.

4.
Single males on Friday nights
most shopping malls forbid.

Stately women swathed in black stride past
headless dolls in mini-skirts behind shop glass.

Handholding in public *haram*—kissing, taboo
of course—also obscene gestures, cursing, spitting.

Static electricity: four years in golden handcuffs,
pressed white collars, stylish ties I wore to school,

my Euro-porn at three a.m. on satellite TV.
Some scenes haunt me, others rouse me still—

in fact, my life in Qatar sometimes pleased me.
Greeting strangers on a stretch of untouched sand,

The peace of God upon you, shaking hands

and wishing peace departing: *Ma'alsalaama*.

Al Samarya

The sheikh's imported masons build the walls
of his museums and riding school
shway, shway, step by step, out into this desert
I am soon to leave—so soon,
by plane away from what
I can't rejoice in anymore.

This desert: I'm crossing it for one last ride,
my mount, Saleem, blinking blowing sand,
picking his way among piled stones
and treacherous hollows,
until he halts and pricks his ears
at rows of date palms in the slanted light.

The farm is a paradise
whose winding track we tread
amid the girth high reeds
where peacocks roost in trees
and peahens brood, where
purple bracts of bougainvillea sprawl
and vines of perfumed jasmine
blot out memories of dust and diesel fumes,
where now beside a newly furrowed field,
at dusk a thumping water pump
sows diamonds through the air.

Pilgrim in my labyrinth,
what progress have I made
turning right, away from what
will soon be left, regretting
what I can't have back?

Salaam, I greet two weary *fellaheen*
on their way to evening prayers.

They wish me peace as well.
Astride my prancing horse
I can't help feeling faintly grand
to have what they have not.
I wish I could apologize.

A peacock flashing blue, alights and cries:
Saleem, alert, is ready, but I hold him
on the bit a moment more.
I walk him past the just lit bird,
then down the track we fly.

III

My Field

The Wayfarer

Which way now? I asked,
uncertain even to whom I was speaking.

Water had risen at my ankles, and the shouts
of those in despair, somewhere to my left,
were growing louder.

Below me—that noise was the sea
pounding where lava oozed spectacularly.

People with phones were recording it all,
transmitting it, preserving it so that others
who wanted it back could keep it
before their eyes, wherever they went.

I took my bearings from the sky:
there was Saturn, dim, but discernible in the south.
I'd heard that the planets would soon line up,
and that they were not against us.

Someone I knew had recently become a ghost—
this, a friend advised, I should deny.

All is deception, I thought, scribbling away
by dawn's early light, a phantasmagoria—
like the dead, projected onto screens.

Still no reply when I called out to the mob,
Which way? Which way?

There were children, wailing, penned nearby,
and when the wind shifted,
the stink of shit-filled diapers was horrific.

One girl, her black eyes imploring;
a boy with scabs on his lips;
an infant sobbing as a blind woman
shoved her thumb into its mouth.

All a deception, I reminded myself.
Ghosts are unreal.
When the stars realign,
astronomers will sigh at their beauty.

After I Died

After I died, there was something about flowers,
a joke about daisies, and then
I was gathering pollen,
                    humming happily at my work
in an infinite field.

What's this pink petaled star?
And what a perfume—
prostrating myself before her majesty,
the lips of her calyx.

It seemed I had always been a little man, but now
I was winged, whisking about Elysium,
my well deserved reward—
                      and with that,
the blooms withered, blossoms fell.

I am a ghost, I thought,
                    clinging to the idea of a body,
whereas before—I couldn't remember.
Wasn't I loved?

I was certain that god didn't exist—not
in the image of a bigger man than me—or maybe
what I actually believed was that god
would have to be more.

I knew not my own capacity, and was that
my fatal flaw?
                Would I be condemned
for choosing to be less than, to be other than?

Then freedom would be an illusion,
I saw,
        an idea
whose flower and fruit ripen and rot,
not a gift, but a sentence—

                          and yet, after I died
a seed remained, a bit of clarity crystalized:
I thought, what if I'd been like him
only pretending to a throne?

What of his honeyed tongue, the errors
he'd wanted to correct, his edicts
too late to revise?
I saw his falsehood as a term
for my own arrogance—

and I forgave him for this.

Arlecchino in the Sky

How I died isn't as interesting as afterwards
this appetite I indulged for paradox.

White noise of the engines, and Death,
my flight attendant
                    serving whisky and peanuts.

I had been craving a forbidden flavor,
and as she glided past, I ran my tongue
on her legs.

Jet-lined at uncanny altitudes
my pleasures seemed satisfied
before they arrived.

The sun rose and the moon rose and the stars never set.
Is this what it means to be alone,
including everyone I've ever loved?

Death, I said, darling, please listen:
confessions come easily to the virtuous,
and I am no great sinner.

Because I Had Nothing to Read

1.
Ah, the ginger and schnapps,
I write on a brown paper napkin.

Then I take stock of my time.
After Mount Tam and the redwoods below,

after Twain's Mysterious Stranger,
O'Connor's Misfit, and the graveyard

dancer, the accordion player in mink
with handcuffs for sale in Key West,

I ride my bike to the White Street Pier
and peer all the way to Havana.

2.
Why don't I belong to the last word
but instead, the first syllable and sound?

Ah, Emily D. must have mused, and refused
to answer except to herself,

the hopeful protagonist in taffeta,
the bird on a globe of glass,

which trifle does the god-king prefer
after his night of shoveling snow?

Hard Words to Say

Time was, and now eventually has arrived.
Only remember can reasonably cry.

Of bayonets, nothing—
displays behind store windows.

Who is a hero in the telephone book?

Days begin to accumulate, and the sand
on sills, curbs and overpasses.

Another person is dead, keep counting.
Justice is a bigger, faster model.

Materiel: a round of ammo.
Ordnance: another sound.

Futures has a certain ring—
Futures is engaged to Wednesday

but Wed and Thursday have a child:
Flesh is weak, but he means well.

Listen, anonymous sources say.
The West Wind you know by name:

it means to change or die.

La Bête is a pussycat, after all.
Butterfly, most difficult to tame.

My Poem
for Mary Gilliland

In my poem
people with love bags
use flea ferries.

I say the horse
and a debit card, I say
that lady has nothing on you.

Okay, you go, okay
in my poem you go,
that's okay too.

In my poem
the dingdong, the cat fish,
the kraut in a jar,

colors of ginger and flesh,
rose and rust and kettle-black,
liver and lime.

I stuff it home.
I can, and I bake, and I
toss my salad with anchovies.

Do you recall the robot-caller
calling about electable
heating coils for the cellar?

What about the Pinot Grigio
our friend drank
from a broken glass?

The blind cat?
The rider, head to toe in black
trackless on the track out back,

the canvas marijuana satchel
scented until Christmas—
it was Thai basil, ho, ho, ho!

In my poem I forget.
In my poem it snows and
I like it six feet deep.

I like gardenias potted
on the balustrades, a long guard rail
and headlights for peace.

In my poem
everybody has more sex forever
and the children are free—free!

In my poem
the antidote, proximity
and a film festival.

In my poem
another archipelago—
but don't you like it here?

Where do you think
your coffee
comes from?

Six Poems after Reading Shoitsu

5 October 2014

There is here no before after.

Now won't become something new.

Forever the leaves refrain from falling.

Where is the sun rising.

November

These last leaves
of maple and box elder,
the black locust finally:
coins and feathers
on the wet lawn.

I rake and sweep
the stepping stones
beside a stream.
In another country
a man clicks his keys and reads
aloud to himself:

These last leaves.

17 Syllables

Fallen leaf: right now
it goes beyond birth and death,
your Buddha Nature.

Warm Blood

You don't know it, but you're
living on a mote of dust,
and your life is the span
of a dust mite's life.

Actually, you do know this,
but you think of yourself
as a mammoth, a saber tooth
tiger killer—or are you

another kind of mammal?

Snow Blind

Look to the right, look to the left,
above you and below you:
a pure white world.

When you have the view make use of it.
If you can't believe your eyes, use mine.

After Shoitsu

The inner light, the outer light
where are they when
you open your eyes?

Asleep, your dreams have
difficult stories to tell;
why can't you accept
the marvelous world
was never born?

What appears like a mirage
is like a mirage,
what appears like a god
is like a god,
and devils wear horns
because you believe in them.

One moment awake is
one more moment of illusion
if you cling to words.

(* Zen master Shoitsu, 1202 – 1280)

To My Cock

Heaven's hawk
and dumb hardware,
star shooter, lazy lout:
                    I can't distinguish us.

Worm or god:
you behold me
never not amused
with my decision
to ignore you or adore you,
brightly, blithely crowing
we are ever young,
and now that time
has had its way with us,
we're growing wise.

                *

At this crossroads
let me heap some stones
to Hermes,
or like a yogi let me lodge
my lingam upright in a yoni.

I believe in your divinity,
my pretty bird, my favorite song,
yet you're hardly more than feathers
and some hollow bones.

                *

Little fish and teapot spout,
how I've treasured you!

Remember when we made a fountain
jetting water out?
Do you remember with me yet

the Christmas gift Erector set,
its tiny bolts and nuts
to fasten struts,
its windup motor
hoisting tiny girders?

You who learned with me
that girls between their legs
have *cookies*—
         so my uncle said—
and with my father
at the circus watched
as flying overhead
a trapeze artist
kicked her pretty legs
as high as we could see.

    *

When you first brought yourself
into my hands, I was an innocent;
your nature never troubled me
until a priest said of our pleasures,
Toilet things are dirty.
Oh, I wanted to be clean and holy then,
renounced our heedless frolicking
and prayed I could stay free of sin—
but like my shadow you returned,
my ever-faithful friend.

    *

Like any other teenage guy
I learned to call you Dick.

Like every guy in love with Jane,
it was Tarzan
at the swimming hole
that I became,

and flexing biceps
yodeled from a tree.

When being funny didn't get me kisses
with my words I won them from the misses.

Later, when a girl who wanted me
asked what name I called you by
I replied, *My cock.*
My cock, she said, and grinned.

       *

Marriage to the one beside me
who has known you best
has taught me better
than to simply set my course
where you,
         my compass needle,
point.

My gift,
     I've said,
trying yet another word
to fit your ever changing form.

Without you, lodestone,
I'd confuse my North and South.

Load reliever,
partner, pal, and confidante,
begetter-of-dreams,

lust is only part of love,
its luster maybe,
        maybe less.
I think you are its instrument,
its flute, its pipe,

its whistle, yes—

yes, I like the sound of that.

Savory

Succulent, juicy, moist
tender, delicious, tasty
appetizing, delectable
exquisite, luscious & sweet.

Also,
saucy
biting
nippy
pungent
sharp & tangy
scathing, cutting & coarse
zesty
salty
peppery
piquant
pungent
racy—

the baroque
pattern of our
conversation.

Then, too,
the recurrence
of certain
percussive
participles:

going & coming
has been & done

went

came.

They Do Our Smoking for Us

People mostly smoke in films or fictions now,
or else in plays when on the stage they light
an inoffensive herbal cigarette,
                              but how
we used to love our 'mels,
and being lovers, shared the hits
when one of us lit up—
                              just saying this
I feel my lungs release
the satisfying smoke that streams
through puckered lips
                              preparing for a kiss.

                    *

My gut says no, you can't do that,
don't dwell on pleasures you've abandoned,
and don't sing the power of tobacco,
even though a store-bought cigarette
still has something in its ruined heart of what
the Old Ones call a *medicine*.

                    *

I often speak to demons, to the people
anyhow who house them, those
who come to me with hopes
I'll hypnotize them out.

Sometimes I tell about what happened
when I found a pack of Camels, nearly full,
outside the Farmer's Market:
I smoked them slowly, one by one,
relieved at last when I was done.

*

I've met quite a few who gave themselves
to other poisons too, heroes, heroines,
surrendering to romance with a partner
claiming they were unafraid of death.
What they wanted was to cure their pain,
for who would willingly wear ball and chain,
as in that ballad, slave to dope or gambling
drink or whores in a house they call the Rising Sun?

But it's a damn good song.

Winter Fields, a Tanka

Winter fields or spring
before the grasses return—
Oh, the wind speaking.

Where do the hills hide sorrow?
Whose bliss does the breeze carry?

Twang

If the archer thinks
the target's center,
distance,
the satisfaction
of a hit,
he is distracted.

The arrow from its bow
departs the string
like so—

it has no aim
yet finds its mark.

Then there's the type of dart
my wife delivered me
today:

the pang I felt,
remorse,
is not a metaphor:

I am to blame.
A thoughtless man.
Exactly.

Waiting for the Hypnotist, Writing in my Program
—at the State Theater, Ithaca

1.
Spring is delayed,
>beginning barely, halting:
>>snowdrops, aconite

and little birds
>named by me
>>among the brambles.

2.
Blackcap briars and multiflora rose,
>bristling privet branches:
>>open places

my cat stalks,
>hunts,
>>haunts.

3.
Two pints
>of black honey.
>>Regret is never sweet

but clots the light
>out of the blossom,
>>the dying cardinal.

4.
Decrease can open corridors
>and canticles:
>>of what is lost

I write—
        not that memory
                can return

a single raindrop to a cloud.

5.
For love he didn't.
        For love she would.

                For love is terrific

and love is tender:
        for her, his love

                was almost home.

6.
And also this I overheard while waiting:
        "Hello,
                mother?"

7.
To write of royalty,
        I would learn
                a formal tongue.

8.
Bravery in common
        with trepidation
                has illusions.

Preparing to abnegate,
        the queen returns
                to her chamber.

A swallow
      nesting in the eaves
            tears her to pieces.

9.
"I heard he never really did
      the research"—
            this behind me in Row B—

and something about degrees,
      the change in Celsius,
            its effect on aging.

10.
Maybe this is worthless too,
      this ink
            running in my brain.

11.
My little black cat
      kills birds
            and eats them

but
      she upchucks
            the undigested parts

which hurts me deeply.

12.
I haven't written yet about
      the current
            running in my hands.

13.
The Ebony Empress: her paws
      are soft leather pads,
           toes furred,

nails furled.

14.
Waiting for the hypnotist,
      jotting in my program,
           and a girl nearby me asks

"Is it real?"

About the Author

Peter Fortunato has published several other poetry collections, the novel *Carnevale* (from Fomite Press) and a memoir, *Desert Wind: My Life in Qatar*. He holds an MFA in Creative Writing from the University of North Carolina at Greensboro, where he was awarded the Randall Jarrell Fellowship, and from Cornell University a BA in English. Mr. Fortunato has taught writing and literature at Cornell and Ithaca College, as well as at Weill Cornell Medicine in Qatar. Among his honors are the Emily Dickinson Prize of the Poetry Society of America, a Pablo Neruda Prize from the Oklahoma Arts Council, and a Yeats Poetry Prize from the WB Yeats Society of NY. Peter Fortunato has been a student of Zen and Tibetan Buddhism for more than 50 years, as well as an artist and practitioner of complementary alternative medicine. He lives in Ithaca, New York.

Acknowledgments

Avocet: "Winter Fields, a Tanka"

Chautauqua: "Good Morning America"

Like Light: 25 Years of Poetry & Prose: "On the Wet Wide Air", "The First Stone"

Metaphysical Times: "1984", "Six Poems after Reading Shoitsu"

My thanks to the Aladdin Poets for their support

Fomite

Writing a review on social media sites for readers will help the progress of independent publishing. To submit a review, go to the book page on any of the sites and follow the links for reviews. Books from independent presses rely on reader-to-reader communications.

For more information or to order any of our books, visit:
http://www.fomitepress.com/our-books.html

More poetry from Fomite...

Anna Blackmer — *Hexagrams*
L. Brown — *Loopholes*
Sue D. Burton — *Little Steel*
Christine Butterworth-McDermott — *Evelyn As*
Christine Butterworth-McDermott — *The Spellbook of Fruit and Flowers*
David Cavanagh— *Cycling in Plato's Cave*
Rajnesh Chakrapani — *The Repetition of Exceptional Weeks*
James Connolly — *Picking Up the Bodies*
Benjamin Dangl — *A World Where Many Worlds Fit*
Greg Delanty — *Behold the Garden*
Greg Delanty — *Loosestrife*
Mason Drukman — *Drawing on Life*
J. C. Ellefson — *Foreign Tales of Exemplum and Woe*
Anna Faktorovich — *Improvisational Arguments*
Peter Fortunato — *World Headquarters*
Barry Goldensohn — *Snake in the Spine, Wolf in the Heart*
Barry Goldensohn — *The Hundred Yard Dash Man*
Barry Goldensohn — *The Listener Aspires to the Condition of Music*
Barry Goldensohn — *Visitors Entrance*
Lorrie Goldensohn — *Little Fish*
R. L. Green — *When You Remember Deir Yassin*
KJ Hannah Greenberg — *Beast There—Don't That*
Kevin Hadduck — *Beloved Brother, Beloved Sister*
John Hawkins — *Mirror to Mirror*
Christopher Heffernan — *[laughter]*
Gail Holst-Warhaft — *Lucky Country*
Judith Kerman — *Definitions*
Yahia Lababidi — *Quarantine Notes*
Joseph Lamport — *Enlightenment*
Raymond Luczak — *A Babble of Objects*
Kate Magill — *Roadworthy Creature, Roadworthy Craft*
Tony Magistrale — *Entanglements*
Gary Mesick — *General Discharge*
Giorigio Mobili — *Sunken Boulevards*

Fomite

Andreas Nolte — *Mascha: The Poems of Mascha Kaléko*
Sherry Olson — *Four-Way Stop*
Brett Ortler — *Lessons of the Dead*
David Polk — *Drinking the River*
Janice Miller Potter — *Meanwell*
Janice Miller Potter — *Thoreau's Umbrella*
Philip Ramp — *Arrivals and Departures*
Philip Ramp — *The Melancholy of a Life as the Joy of Living It Slowly Chills*
Joseph D. Reich — *A Case Study of Werewolves*
Joseph D. Reich — *Connecting the Dots to Shangrila*
Joseph D. Reich — *The Derivation of Cowboys and Indians*
Joseph D. Reich — *The Hole That Runs Through Utopia*
Joseph D. Reich — *The Housing Market*
Kenneth Rosen and Richard Wilson — *Gomorrah*
Fred Rosenblum — *Of Our Elaborate Plans*
Fred Rosenblum — *Playing Chicken with an Iron Horse*
Fred Rosenblum — *Tramping Solo*
Fred Rosenblum — *Vietnumb*
David Schein — *My Murder and Other Local News*
Harold Schweizer — *Miriam's Book*
Scott T. Starbuck — *Carbonfish Blues*
Scott T. Starbuck — *Hawk on Wire*
Scott T. Starbuck — *Industrial Oz*
Seth Steinzor — *Among the Lost*
Seth Steinzor — *Once Was Lost*
Seth Steinzor — *To Join the Lost*
Susan Thomas — *In the Sadness Museum*
Susan Thomas — *Silent Acts of Public Indiscretion*
Susan Thomas — *The Empty Notebook Interrogates Itself*
Sharon Webster — *Everyone Lives Here*
Tony Whedon — *The Tres Riches Heures*
Tony Whedon — *The Falkland Quartet*
Claire Zoghb — *Dispatches from Everest*

www.ingramcontent.com/pod-product-compliance
Lightning Source LLC
Chambersburg PA
CBHW021653120626
46545CB00002B/844